D0581722

GOOD HOUSEKEEPING

EASY
ENTERTAINING

Planning a dinner party? Throwing a special meal for the family? Or just having a few friends round for a cosy dinner? You needn't be daunted by the prospect or stuck for ideas. Simply turn the pages of this book and you'll find an absolute host of wonderful, inspiring ways to make special occasion food—from the wickedly extravagant and exotic to budget-conscious dishes that look and taste expensive. The clear step-by-step illustrations take you through the methods without a hitch.

With the compliments of

COOKERY NOTES

Follow either metric or imperial measures for the recipes in this book as they are not interchangeable. Sets of spoon measures are available in both metric and imperial size to give accurate measurement of small quantities. All spoon measures are level unless otherwise stated. When measuring milk we have used the exact conversion of 568 ml (1 pint).

* Size 2 eggs should be used except when otherwise stated.
† Granulated sugar is used unless otherwise stated.
● Plain flour is used unless otherwise stated.

OVEN TEMPERATURE CHART

°C	°F	Gas mark
110	225	$\frac{1}{4}$
130	250	$\frac{1}{2}$
140	275	1
150	300	2
170	325	3
180	350	4
190	375	5
200	400	6
220	425	7
230	450	8
240	475	9

METRIC CONVERSION SCALE

LIQUID			SOLID		
Imperial	Exact conversion	Recommended ml	Imperial	Exact conversion	Recommended g
$\frac{1}{4}$ pint	142 ml	150 ml	1 oz	28.35 g	25 g
$\frac{1}{2}$ pint	284 ml	300 ml	2 oz	56.7 g	50 g
1 pint	568 ml	600 ml	4 oz	113.4 g	100 g
$1\frac{1}{2}$ pints	851 ml	900 ml	8 oz	226.8 g	225 g
$1\frac{3}{4}$ pints	992 ml	1 litre	12 oz	340.2 g	350 g
For quantities of $1\frac{3}{4}$ pints and over, litres and fractions of a litre have been used.			14 oz	397.0 g	400 g
			16 oz (1 lb)	453.6 g	450 g
			1 kilogram (kg) equals 2.2 lb.		

Illustrated on the cover: Filet De Boeuf En Croûte (page 12)

KEY TO SYMBOLS

1.00* Indicates minimum preparation and cooking times in hours and minutes. They do not include prepared items in the list of ingredients; calculated times apply only to the method. An asterisk * indicates extra time should be allowed, so check the note below symbols.

Chef's hats indicate degree of difficulty of a recipe: no hat means it is straightforward; one hat slightly more complicated; two hats indicates that it is for more advanced cooks.

£ Indicates a recipe which is good value for money; £ £ indicates an expensive recipe. No £ sign indicates an inexpensive recipe.

✳ Indicates that a recipe will freeze. If there is no symbol, the recipe is unsuitable for freezing. An asterisk * indicates special freezer instructions so check the note immediately below the symbols.

309 cals Indicates calories per serving, including any suggestions (e.g. cream, to serve) given in the ingredients.

GOOD HOUSEKEEPING

EASY ENTERTAINING

Contents

WATERCRESS SOUP

| 0.25 | £ | ✳ | 325 cals |

Serves 4

100 g (4 oz) butter or margarine

1 medium onion, skinned and chopped

2 bunches watercress

50 g (2 oz) plain flour

750 ml (1¼ pints) chicken or veal stock

300 ml (½ pint) milk

salt and freshly ground pepper

1 Melt the butter in a saucepan, add the onion and cook gently for 10 minutes until soft but not coloured.

2 Meanwhile, wash and trim the watercress, leaving some of the stem, then chop roughly.

3 Add the chopped watercress to the onion, cover the pan with a lid and cook gently for a further 4 minutes.

4 Add the flour and cook gently, stirring, for 1–2 minutes. Remove from the heat and gradually blend in the stock and milk. Bring to the boil, stirring constantly then, simmer for 3 minutes. Season to taste.

5 Sieve or purée the soup in a blender or food processor. Return to the rinsed-out pan and reheat gently, without boiling. Taste and adjust seasoning, if necessary. Serve hot.

CREAM OF CARROT WITH ORANGE SOUP

| 0.55 | ⬭ | ✳ | 73–110 cals |

Serves 4–6

25 g (1 oz) butter or margarine

700 g (1½ lb) carrots, peeled and sliced

225 g (8 oz) onion, skinned and sliced

1 litre (1¾ pints) chicken or ham stock

salt and freshly ground pepper

1 orange

1 Melt the butter in a saucepan, add the vegetables and cook gently for 10 minutes until softened slightly.

2 Add the stock and bring to the boil. Lower the heat, cover and simmer for about 40 minutes, or until the vegetables are tender.

3 Sieve or purée the vegetables with half of the stock in a blender or food processor. Add this mixture to the stock remaining in the pan.

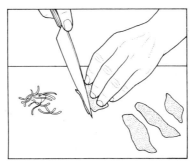

4 Meanwhile, pare half of the orange rind thinly, using a potato peeler, then cut it into shreds. Cook the shreds in gently boiling water until tender.

5 Finely grate the remaining orange rind into the soup. Stir well to combine with the ingredients in the pan.

6 Squeeze the juice of the orange into the pan. Reheat the soup gently, then taste and adjust seasoning. Drain the shreds of orange rind and use to garnish the soup just before serving. Serve hot.

VEGETABLE TERRINE

| 2.30 | 🍴🍴 | £ | 250–334 cals |

Serves 6–8

- 900 g (2 lb) turnips, peeled and cut into chunks
- 450 g (1 lb) carrots, peeled and sliced
- 450 g (1 lb) fresh spinach, trimmed, or 300 g (10.6 oz) packet frozen spinach
- 50 g (2 oz) butter or margarine
- 1 medium onion, skinned and thinly sliced
- 350 g (12 oz) flat mushrooms, sliced
- finely grated rind and juice of $\frac{1}{2}$ lemon
- 4 eggs
- salt and freshly ground white pepper
- 1.25 ml ($\frac{1}{4}$ tsp) ground coriander
- 1.25 ml ($\frac{1}{4}$ tsp) freshly grated nutmeg
- 30 ml (2 tbsp) chopped fresh parsley
- 2 ripe tomatoes, skinned
- 300 ml ($\frac{1}{2}$ pint) Vinaigrette

1 Put the turnips into a medium saucepan, cover with cold water and bring to the boil. Lower the heat and simmer for 10–15 minutes, until completely tender.

2 Meanwhile, put the carrots in a separate saucepan and cover with cold water. Bring to the boil and cook for 10 minutes or until completely tender. Drain both turnips and carrots.

3 Wash the fresh spinach in several changes of cold water. Place in a saucepan with only the water that clings to the leaves. Cook gently for 5 minutes until wilted, 7–10 minutes if using frozen spinach. Drain well.

4 Melt 40 g (1½ oz) of the butter in a frying pan, add the onion and fry gently for about 10 minutes until very soft. Add the mushrooms and fry, stirring constantly, for a further 5 minutes. Stir in the lemon rind and juice.

5 Put the mushroom mixture in a blender or food processor and work until smooth. Transfer to a small heavy-based pan. Cook over moderate heat, stirring constantly, until all the liquid has evaporated and the purée is fairly thick and dry. Watch that the mixture does not catch and burn.

6 Purée and dry the turnips, carrots and spinach in the same way and place each purée in a separate bowl. Add 1 egg to each purée and mix well. Season each with salt and pepper to taste. Stir the coriander into the carrot purée, the grated nutmeg into the spinach and the chopped parsley into the mushroom.

7 Brush a 1.1 litre (2 pint) terrine or loaf tin with the remaining butter. Put a layer of turnip purée in the bottom, making sure it is quite level. Cover with a layer of carrot, followed by spinach and finally mushroom. Cover the tin tightly with foil.

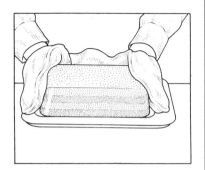

8 Place the terrine in a roasting tin and pour in enough hot water to come three-quarters of the way up the sides of the terrine. Bake in the oven at 180°C (350°F) mark 4 for 1 hour 20 minutes or until firm. Remove and allow to cool slightly, then turn out carefully on to a serving plate.

9 Just before serving, put the tomatoes and vinaigrette in a blender or food processor and work until smooth. Do not let the dressing stand before serving or it will separate.

10 Serve the terrine hot or cold, cut into slices, on top of the tomato vinaigrette.

Note Other vegetables may be used when in season, such as cauliflower, fennel, watercress, parsnips and even peas. Try to balance colour and flavour.

PRAWN AND GRUYÈRE COCOTTES

| 0.35 | £ £ | 449 cals |

Serves 4

15 g (½ oz) butter

15 ml (1 tbsp) olive or vegetable oil

1 small onion, skinned and finely chopped

4 rashers of back bacon, rinded and chopped

350 g (12 oz) peeled prawns, defrosted and thoroughly dried if frozen

150 ml (¼ pint) soured cream

1 egg, beaten

salt and freshly ground pepper

100 g (4 oz) Gruyère, grated

1 Melt the butter with the oil in a heavy-based saucepan, add the onion and fry gently for 5 minutes until soft but not coloured.

2 Add the bacon and fry until turning colour, stirring frequently. Add the prawns, increase the heat and stir fry for 5 minutes.

3 Transfer the mixture to the bowl, add the soured cream and egg and salt and pepper to taste. Mix well.

4 Divide the mixture equally between 4 cocottes or ramekins. Sprinkle with Gruyère. Bake in the oven at 190°C (375°F) mark 5 for 15 minutes until golden and bubbling. Serve hot.

PRAWN AND GRUYÈRE COCOTTES

The majority of Gruyère comes from Switzerland. Although the French also make Gruyère cheese, there is not enough for export, so it is unlikely you will see it for sale outside France. Both cheeses have a similar, slightly fruity, flavour, which comes from the fact that the cows graze in lush alpine pastures. Fresh Gruyère is an excellent table cheese, although the majority of Gruyère is used in cooking, for its unique melting qualities. Swiss Emmental can be used instead of Gruyère in any recipe; it has larger holes and a milder flavour.

BLINI (RUSSIAN BUCKWHEAT PANCAKES)

| 1.30 | 🗄 £ £ ✳ | 88 cals |

Makes 24

300 ml (½ pint) milk

2.5 ml (½ tsp) dried yeast

2.5 ml (½ tsp) sugar

125 g (4 oz) plain flour

125 g (4 oz) buckwheat or wholemeal flour

1 egg, separated

15 g (½ oz) butter, melted

pinch of salt

vegetable oil for frying

2 hard-boiled eggs

1 medium onion, skinned and finely chopped

150 ml (¼ pint) soured cream or smetana

caviar or lumpfish roe

1 Warm the milk to blood temperature. Stir in the dried yeast and sugar. Leave in a warm place for 15–20 minutes or until beginning to froth.

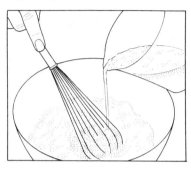

2 Mix the flours together in a bowl. Gradually beat in the milk mixture to form a smooth, thick batter. Cover and leave again in a warm place until doubled in size, about 40 minutes.

3 Beat in the egg yolk, melted butter and salt. Whisk the egg white until stiff and fold into the batter mixture until evenly incorporated.

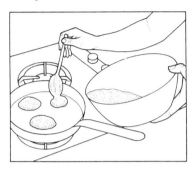

4 Lightly oil a non-stick frying pan. Place over moderate heat. Drop small spoonfuls of batter into the pan. Cook for about 2–3 minutes until bubbles form.

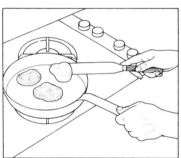

5 Turn the pancakes over with a palette knife and cook for a further 1 minute until golden brown. Keep warm between layers of greaseproof paper in a low oven until all the batter is cooked.

6 Serve the blini with finely chopped hard-boiled egg, chopped onion, spoonfuls of soured cream and caviar or lumpfish roe.

FRESH HADDOCK MOUSSE

0.40* ☐ £ £ 359 cals

* plus 30 minutes cooling, 2 hours
chilling and 30 minutes to come to
room temperature

Serves 6

350 g (12 oz) fresh haddock fillet

200 ml (7 fl oz) milk

1 bay leaf

6 peppercorns

salt and freshly ground pepper

25 g (1 oz) butter or margarine

30 ml (2 tbsp) plain flour

7.5 ml (1½ tsp) gelatine

15 ml (1 tbsp) Dijon mustard

5 ml (1 tsp) tomato purée

5 ml (1 tsp) Worcestershire sauce

90 ml (6 tbsp) double cream

150 ml (¼ pint) mayonnaise

15 ml (1 tbsp) lemon juice

cucumber, to garnish

1 Place the haddock in a sauté
or frying pan. Pour in the milk
and add the bay leaf, peppercorns
and a good pinch of salt. Bring
slowly to the boil, cover and
simmer for 5–10 minutes, or until
the fish flakes easily when tested
with a fork.

2 Strain the cooking liquid from
the fish and reserve. Skin and
flake the flesh, discarding any
bones.

3 Melt the butter in a saucepan,
add the flour and cook gently,
stirring for 1–2 minutes. Remove
from the heat and gradually blend
in the strained cooked liquid.
Bring to the boil, stirring constantly, then simmer for 3
minutes until thick and smooth.
Remove the pan from the heat and
sprinkle in the gelatine. Stir
briskly until dissolved.

4 Work the sauce in a blender or
food processor with the fish,
mustard, tomato purée,
Worcestershire sauce and salt and
pepper to taste. Transfer to a bowl
and leave to cool for 30 minutes.

5 Lightly whip the cream and
stir it into the fish mixture
with the mayonnaise and lemon
juice. Check the seasoning.

6 Spoon the mousse into 6
individual ramekins or soufflé
dishes and chill in the refrigerator
for at least 2 hours until set. Leave
at cool room temperature for 30
minutes before serving, garnished
with cucumber.

TURMERIC AND WALNUT MUSHROOMS

| 0.15* | £ £ | 514 cals |

* plus 8 hours chilling

Serves 8

1.1 kg (2½ lb) button mushrooms

300 ml (½ pint) olive or vegetable oil

100 ml (4 fl oz) white wine vinegar

5 ml (1 tsp) Dijon mustard

5 ml (1 tsp) caster sugar

15 ml (1 tbsp) ground turmeric

1 garlic clove, skinned and crushed

salt and freshly ground pepper

125 g (4 oz) walnut pieces

350 g (12 oz) Emmental, cubed

chopped fresh parsley, to garnish

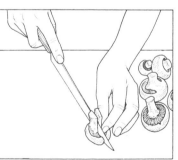

1 Wipe the button mushrooms. Leave the small ones whole and cut any larger ones in half. Put in a serving dish.

2 In a jug, whisk together the oil, vinegar, mustard, sugar, turmeric and crushed garlic until well blended into a dressing. Add salt and pepper to taste.

3 Pour the turmeric dressing over the mushrooms and mix thoroughly to coat. Cover and leave to marinate in the refrigerator for at least 8 hours.

4 To serve, stir the mushrooms well and mix in the walnut pieces and Emmental. Garnish with chopped parsley.

11

FILET DE BOEUF EN CROÛTE
(BEEF WELLINGTON)

2.00	🥘	£ £	938 cals

Serves 6

1.4 kg (3 lb) fillet of beef

2 garlic cloves, skinned and cut into thin slivers (optional)

15 g ($\frac{1}{2}$ oz) butter

30 ml (2 tbsp) olive oil

30 ml (2 tbsp) brandy

salt and freshly ground pepper

600 g ($1\frac{1}{4}$ lb) puff pastry, thawed if frozen

100 g (4 oz) pâté de foie gras, at room temperature

beaten egg, to glaze

90 ml (6 tbsp) Madeira, port or dry sherry

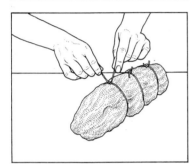

1 Trim any fat off the beef and tie into a neat, regular shape with trussing thread or string.

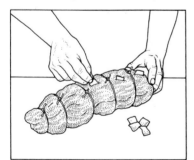

2 With a sharp pointed knife, make shallow incisions all over the meat at regular intervals. Insert the garlic slivers into the incisions.

3 Melt the butter with the oil in a flameproof casserole or large, heavy-based frying pan. Add the meat and fry over moderate heat until well browned and sealed on all sides. Roast in the oven at 200°C (400°F) mark 6 for 15 minutes.

4 Warm the brandy in a small separate pan or a ladle. Remove the pan containing the meat from the oven, pour over the brandy and ignite.

5 When the flames have died down, lift the meat out of the pan and set aside on a plate until cold. Reserve the juices in the pan.

6 Meanwhile, roll out the pastry on a lightly floured surface to a rectangle measuring 45 × 30 cm (18 × 12 inches).

7 Remove the thread or string from the cold meat. Soften the pâté with a knife, then spread over the top and sides of the meat. Sprinkle with salt and pepper.

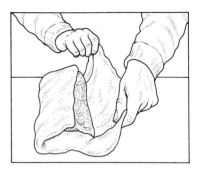

8 Place the meat on the pastry, Pâté side down. Wrap pastry around the meat, sealing the joins with water.

9 Invert the meat and place join side down on a dampened baking sheet. Decorate with any leftover pastry trimmings, sticking them on with water. Brush all over the pastry with beaten egg.

10 Bake in the oven at 200°C (400°F) mark 6 for 55–60 minutes, according to how well done you like your beef.

11 Meanwhile, make the gravy. Pour the Madeira into the pan in which the meat was sealed. Add 600 ml (1 pint) water and bring to the boil, stirring to scrape up any sediment in the pan. Boil until reduced slightly, then remove from the heat and taste and adjust seasoning.

12 At the end of the cooking time, turn off the oven and leave the meat to 'rest' for 15 minutes before serving. Reheat the gravy at the last moment and pour into a sauceboat. Transfer the fillet whole, to a serving plate and carve the meat at the table.

STEAK DIANE

| 0.60 | £ | 318 cals |

Serves 4

25 g (1 oz) butter or margarine

15 ml (1 tbsp) vegetable oil

4 minute steaks

2 shallots, skinned and finely
    chopped

30 ml (2 tbsp) brandy

15 ml (1 tbsp) Worcestershire
    sauce

10 ml (2 tsp) meat stock

15 ml (1 tbsp) tomato purée

30 ml (2 tbsp) chopped fresh
    parsley

1 Melt the butter with the oil in a heavy-based frying pan. When foaming, add the steaks and fry for 1 minute on each side.

2 Add the shallots and pour in the brandy. Remove from the heat and ignite the pan juices. Let the flames die down and stir in the Worcestershire sauce, meat stock, tomato purée and 15 ml (1 tbsp) cold water.

3 Increase the heat and shake the pan to mix the sauces together. Add the parsley and bring to the boil. Serve immediately, straight from the pan.

STEAK DIANE

Steak Diane is not French, but Australian! It was invented by a chef in an Australian restaurant, where it is always prepared by the head waiter at the table. The authentic recipe is made with a demi-glace sauce, but it is unlikely that any cook other than a restaurant chef will have this to hand. Instead, use meat stock as suggested in this recipe. You will find the results extremely good.

BEEF IN BRANDY AND MUSTARD

| 2.00 | £ £ ✳* | 477 cals |

* freeze before step 4

Serves 6

1.1-kg (2½-lb) piece chuck steak
30 ml (2 tbsp) vegetable oil
50 g (2 oz) butter
2 onions, skinned and chopped
60 ml (4 tbsp) brandy
1 garlic clove, skinned and crushed
15 ml (1 tbsp) whole grain mustard
300 ml (½ pint) beef stock
salt and freshly ground pepper
225 g (8 oz) celery, trimmed
50 g (2 oz) walnut halves
75 ml (5 tbsp) single cream

1 Cut the piece of chuck steak into thin strips about 0.5 cm (¼ inch) wide and 3.5 cm (1½ inches) long.

2 Heat the oil with 25 g (1 oz) butter in a medium flameproof casserole and brown the meat well; take out and drain.

3 Add the onion to the reheated pan juices and fry until golden; return the meat to the casserole and flame with the brandy. Stir in garlic with mustard, stock and seasoning and bring to the boil.

4 Cover the dish tightly and cook in the oven at 150°C (300°F) mark 2 for about 1½ hours or until the meat is quite tender.

5 Cut the celery diagonally into fine strips and, just before serving time, sauté with the walnuts in the remaining butter until golden.

6 Add the walnut mixture to the meat and bring to the boil, stirring; simmer for 2–3 minutes and drizzle cream over the top before serving.

MIDDLE EASTERN MEATBALLS WITH AUBERGINE AND TOMATO

| 1.30* | 🍳 | ✳ | 415 cals |

* plus 30 minutes degorging
aubergines and 1 hour chilling

Serves 6

2 medium aubergines, about 450 g
(1 lb) total weight, sliced

salt and freshly ground pepper

150 ml ($\frac{1}{4}$ pint) vegetable oil

450 g (1 lb) boneless lamb

2 thick slices of white bread,
crusts removed

1 small onion, skinned

10 ml (2 tsp) ground cumin

450 g (1 lb) tomatoes, skinned and
chopped

15 ml (1 tbsp) tomato purée

450 ml ($\frac{3}{4}$ pint) chicken stock or dry
white wine and water, mixed

2.5 ml ($\frac{1}{2}$ tsp) ground allspice

450 ml ($\frac{3}{4}$ pint) vegetable oil, for
deep-frying

chopped fresh parsley, to serve

1 Layer the aubergine slices in a
colander, sprinkling each layer
with salt. Cover with a plate,
weight down and leave for 30
minutes to draw out moisture.

2 Drain the aubergine slices,
rinse and dry well. In a large
frying pan, fry for 4–5 minutes in
batches in the oil, turning once.
Drain the fried aubergines on
absorbent kitchen paper.

3 Put the lamb through the
blades of a mincer twice with
the fried aubergines, bread and
onion. (Or work the ingredients in
a food processor.)

4 In a bowl, mix the minced
meat with the cumin and
seasoning to taste, then chill in the
refrigerator for about 30 minutes,
until firm.

5 Meanwhile, put the tomatoes,
tomato purée, stock and
allspice in a large flameproof
casserole with seasoning to taste.
Bring to the boil, stirring to break
up the tomatoes, then lower the
heat and simmer while making
the meatballs.

6 With floured hands, form the
mixture into 30 walnut-sized
balls. Chill in the refrigerator for
30 minutes to firm.

7 Heat the oil for deep-frying to
190°C (375°F). Add the meatballs in batches and fry until
browned on all sides. Remove
with a slotted spoon and drain on
absorbent kitchen paper.

8 Add the drained meatballs to
the tomato sauce then cover
and simmer gently for 30 minutes,
shaking the casserole frequently
so that the meatballs become
saturated in the sauce.

9 Taste and, if necessary, adjust
the seasoning of the tomato
sauce before serving. Garnish with
chopped fresh parsley.

MIDDLE EASTERN MEATBALLS

Lamb, aubergines and tomatoes
are a popular combination of
ingredients in Middle Eastern
cookery. Here the lamb and
aubergines are minced together
to make meatballs, an unusual
method, but one which gives a
tasty, moist result. To save time,
buy ready-minced lamb, but
make sure it is fairly lean, or
the fat will run out into the sauce
and make the dish unpalatable.

GOSHT BIRYANI
(SPICED LAMB AND RICE CASSEROLE)

| 2.00 | 🍴 f | 710 cals |

Serves 6

450 g (1 lb) basmati rice

1 medium onion, skinned and roughly chopped

2 garlic cloves, skinned

2.5 cm (1 inch) piece of fresh root ginger, peeled and roughly chopped

150 ml ($\frac{1}{4}$ pint) ghee or vegetable oil

450 g (1 lb) boned shoulder of lamb, trimmed of excess fat and cut into 2.5 cm (1 inch) cubes

150 ml ($\frac{1}{4}$ pint) natural yogurt

50 g (2 oz) ground almonds

4 whole cloves

2 black cardamoms

4 green cardamoms

5 ml (1 tsp) cumin seeds

2.5 cm (1 inch) stick cinnamon or 4 pieces of cassia bark

50 g (2 oz) sultanas

5–10 ml (1–2 tsp) salt

large pinch of saffron threads, or 3 ml (1 tsp) each yellow and orange food colourings

3 ml (1 tsp) rose water

crisp browned onions, to garnish

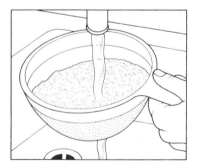

1 Put the rice in a sieve and wash well under cold running water until the water runs clear. Transfer the rice to a bowl, cover with cold water and leave to soak.

2 Meanwhile, put the onion, garlic and ginger in a blender or food processor and work until smooth. Set aside.

3 Heat 60 ml (4 tbsp) of the ghee in a large flameproof casserole. Add the cubes of lamb and fry over high heat until well browned on all sides. Transfer to a plate with a slotted spoon.

4 Add the onion purée to the residual ghee in the pan and fry over high heat for 2 minutes, stirring constantly. Return the meat to the pan, then stir in the yogurt 1 spoonful at a time. Cook each addition over high heat, stirring constantly, until the yogurt is absorbed.

5 Add the ground almonds and 150 ml ($\frac{1}{4}$ pint) water. Bring to the boil, cover and simmer gently for 30 minutes, stirring occasionally to prevent sticking.

6 Heat another 60 ml (4 tbsp) ghee in a large heavy-based frying pan, add the cloves, cardamom pods, cumin seeds and cinnamon and fry gently for 1 minute.

7 Drain the rice well and add to the spices, stirring until the rice absorbs all the fat. Stir in the sultanas and salt to taste.

8 Sprinkle the spiced rice evenly over the meat in the casserole. Carefully pour in enough water to just cover the rice. DO NOT STIR. Bring to the boil, cover and bake in the oven at 150°C (300°F) mark 2 for 30 minutes.

9 Meanwhile, if using saffron threads, soak them in 60 ml (4 tbsp) boiling water.

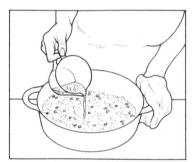

10 Remove the casserole from the oven, uncover and drizzle over the saffron water or food colourings. Recover tightly and bake for 15 minutes.

11 To serve, uncover the biryani and carefully fork up the meat and rice. Sprinkle with the rose water and, finally, the onion garnish.

PORK LOIN WITH CIDER

| 2.40 | 🍳 🍳 £ £ | 926 cals |

Serves 6

600 ml (1 pint) dry cider

1.8 kg (4 lb) loin of pork, boned,
   with rind on

salt

2 onions, skinned

125 g (4 oz) rindless streaky bacon

50 g (2 oz) butter

225 g (8 oz) button or cup
   mushrooms, wiped and chopped

5 ml (1 tsp) dried rubbed sage

125 g (4 oz) fresh white
   breadcrumbs

1 egg, beaten

freshly ground pepper

30 ml (2 tbsp) vegetable oil

175 g (6 oz) carrots, peeled and
   cut into matchsticks

2 bay leaves

15 ml (1 tbsp) cornflour

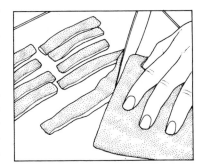

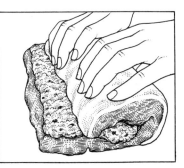

1 Pour the cider into a small pan and boil to reduce by half. Remove the rind and most of the fat from the pork and cut into thin fingers. Place these in a small roasting tin. Add salt; set aside.

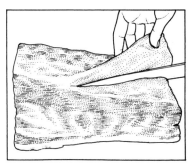

2 Slit the loin of pork along the eye of the meat three-quarters of the way through, from the centre outwards. Open out so that it forms a long roll.

3 To make the stuffing, chop one of the onions and snip the bacon into small pieces.

4 Melt half the butter in a medium frying pan, add the bacon and onion and cook slowly until the bacon fat runs and the ingredients begin to brown. Increase the heat, add the mushrooms and cook until all excess moisture has evaporated.

5 Turn out into a large bowl and stir in the sage, breadcrumbs and enough egg to bind. Season, mix well and cool.

6 Spread the cold stuffing over the pork, roll up and tie at regular intervals. Slice the remaining onion. Heat the oil in a flameproof casserole, add the remaining butter and brown the joint. Remove from pan.

7 Add the sliced onion and carrots to the residual fat and lightly brown. Replace the meat and pour the reduced cider around. Stir in the bay leaves and seasoning and bring to the boil.

8 Cover tightly and place on a low shelf in the oven at 170°C (325°F) mark 3. Place the roasting tin of pork rind and fat above and cook both for about 2 hours.

9 Lift the pork out of the casserole with any stuffing that has oozed out and slice, discarding string. Remove vegetables from casserole and arrange on the serving plate with the sliced pork, cover and keep warm.

10 Mix the cornflour to a smooth paste with a little water and stir into the pan juices. Bring to the boil, stirring. Cook for 2 minutes. To serve, garnish with the crackling strips. Serve the gravy separately.

WHOLE CHICKEN COOKED WITH YOGURT AND SPICES

1.30* 〔 **390 cals**

* plus 2 hours marinating

Serves 4

1.4 kg (3 lb) chicken

60 ml (4 tbsp) lemon or lime juice

2 garlic cloves, skinned and finely
    chopped

2.5 cm (1 inch) piece of fresh root
    ginger, peeled and finely
    chopped

10 ml (2 tsp) ground cumin

10 ml (2 tsp) ground coriander

5 ml (1 tsp) garam masala

10 ml (2 tsp) salt

2.5 ml ($\frac{1}{2}$ tsp) freshly ground
    pepper

45 ml (3 tbsp) ghee or vegetable
    oil

2 medium onions, skinned and
    finely sliced

5 ml (1 tsp) turmeric

2.5 ml ($\frac{1}{2}$ tsp) cayenne

300 ml ($\frac{1}{2}$ pint) natural yogurt

50 g (2 oz) unsalted cashew nuts or
    blanched almonds

chopped fresh coriander,
    to garnish

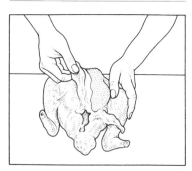

1 Skin the chicken completely, leaving it whole. With a sharp knife, make small incisions all over the bird. Place in a large bowl.

2 Mix the lemon juice with the garlic, ginger, cumin, coriander, garam masala, salt and pepper. Rub all over the chicken, working the mixture into the incisions. Cover and leave to marinate in the refrigerator for about 2 hours.

3 Heat the ghee in a frying pan, add the onions and fry gently for 8–10 minutes until soft and golden brown. Add the tumeric and cayenne and fry for a further 2 minutes.

4 Add the yogurt, 15 ml (1 tbsp) at a time. Cook each addition over high heat, stirring constantly, until the yogurt is absorbed.

5 Transfer the onion and yogurt mixture to a blender or food processor. Add the cashew nuts and work until smooth.

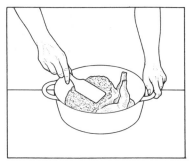

6 Place the chicken in a casserole or roasting tin and spread the onion mixture all over the bird. Cover with a lid or foil, then bake in the oven at 180°C (350°F) mark 4, basting frequently, for about 1 hour or until the chicken is tender.

7 Transfer the chicken to a warmed serving dish and spoon over the sauce. Sprinkle with the chopped coriander and serve immediately.

CHICKEN POT PIES

3.00*	✳*	847 cals

* plus cooling overnight; freeze without pastry glaze in step 10

Serves 4

1.1 kg (2½ lb) chicken, giblets removed

1 lemon

few sprigs of fresh tarragon or 2.5 ml (½ tsp) dried

1 bay leaf

salt and freshly ground pepper

2 leeks, trimmed and sliced

2 large carrots, peeled and thinly sliced

175 g (6 oz) button onions, topped and tailed

40 g (1½ oz) butter or margarine

175 g (6 oz) button mushrooms, wiped and halved or sliced if large

45 ml (3 tbsp) plain flour

60 ml (4 tbsp) double cream

368 g (13 oz) packet frozen puff pastry, thawed

a little beaten egg, to glaze

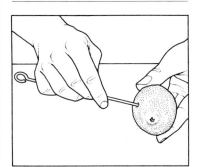

1 Wash the chicken inside and out. Prick the lemon all over with a skewer, then place inside the chicken.

2 Put the chicken in a large saucepan with the tarragon, bay leaf and seasoning to taste. Add the giblets (except the liver), then pour in just enough water to cover the chicken and bring slowly to the boil. Lower the heat, half cover with a lid and simmer for 1¼ hours or until tender.

3 Add the leeks and carrots for the last 30 minutes of the cooking time. Remove the pan from the heat and leave the chicken and vegetables to cool in the liquid.

4 Remove the chicken from the cooking liquid. Cut the flesh from the bird, discarding all skin and bones. Dice the flesh into bite-sized pieces. Set aside.

5 Place the button onions in a bowl, pour in boiling water to cover and leave for 2–3 minutes. Drain and plunge into cold water, then remove the onions one at a time and peel off the skins with your fingers.

6 Melt the butter or margarine in a clean saucepan, add the onions and fry gently for 5 minutes until lightly coloured.

7 Strain the cooking liquid from the chicken, measure and reserve 300 ml (½ pint). Add the mushrooms to the onions, together with the leeks and carrots, discarding the tarragon sprigs, if used, and the bay leaf. Fry the vegetables gently for 1–2 minutes, then add the chicken pieces and fry for a few minutes more.

8 Mix the flour to a paste with the cream. Gradually blend in the measured cooking liquid, then pour into the pan of chicken and vegetables. Add seasoning to taste. Simmer, stirring, for 2–3 minutes, then turn into four 300 ml (½ pint) ovenproof pie dishes. Cover and leave until completely cold, overnight if convenient.

9 Roll out the pastry on a floured surface and cut out four circles or ovals to make lids. Cut four strips of pastry long enough to go around the rims of the dishes.

10 Dampen the rims of the pie dishes then place the strips of pastry around them. Dampen the pastry strips, then place the circles of pastry on top. Press firmly to seal, then knock up and flute. Make a hole in the centre of each pie and decorate with pastry trimmings if liked. Glaze with beaten egg.

11 Bake the pies in the oven at 200°C (400°F) mark 6 for 25 minutes or until the pastry is golden brown and the filling heated through. Serve hot.

CHEESE AND ANCHOVY GRILLED CHICKEN BREASTS

| 1.00 | £ £ | 511 cals |

Serves 6

50 g (2 oz) can anchovy fillets in oil

30 ml (2 tbsp) finely chopped onion

5 ml (1 tsp) lemon juice

6 chicken breasts

vegetable oil, for brushing

225 g (8 oz) Mozzarella cheese, sliced

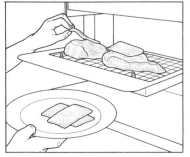

1 Drain 15 ml (1 tbsp) of the oil from the anchovy can into a small saucepan. Chop the anchovies finely.

2 Heat the anchovy oil, add the anchovies and onion and cook for about 5 minutes, until a paste forms. Stir in the lemon juice, then remove from the heat and leave to cool.

3 Lift the skin from each chicken breast and rub 5 ml (1 tsp) of the anchovy mixture on the flesh underneath the skin.

4 Put the chicken pieces, skin side down, on to a rack placed over the grill pan. Grill under moderate heat for 35–45 minutes until tender, turning once. Brush with oil occasionally during cooking, to moisten.

5 Cover the chicken breasts with slices of cheese and grill for a further 5 minutes, or until the cheese begins to bubble.

CHEESE AND ANCHOVY GRILLED CHICKEN BREASTS

Anchovies tend to be rather salty. If you have the time when preparing this dish, it helps to soak the anchovies first, to remove excess salt. Simply drain the oil from the can, then place the anchovy fillets in a shallow dish. Pour over just enough milk to cover, then leave to soak for 20–30 minutes. Drain thoroughly and pat dry. The anchovies are now ready for use.

CASSEROLED TURKEY IN RED WINE

| 3.20* | ✳ | 434–495 cals |

* plus 2–3 hours cooling

Serves 4

25 g (1 oz) butter

30 ml (2 tbsp) vegetable oil

450–700 g (1–1½ lb) turkey casserole meat

125 g (4 oz) lean streaky bacon, rinded and diced

30 ml (2 tbsp) plain flour

good pinch of dried thyme

1 bay leaf

150 ml (¼ pint) red wine

300 ml (½ pint) water (or unseasoned stock)

salt and freshly ground pepper

12 small onions or shallots, skinned

chopped fresh parsley and pastry crescents or croûtons, to serve

1 Melt half the butter with half the oil in a large frying pan. When foaming, add the turkey meat and brown well. Remove with a slotted spoon and place in a casserole.

2 Add the bacon to the frying pan and fry until beginning to brown. Remove the bacon with a slotted spoon and add to the turkey.

3 Stir the flour, thyme and bay leaf into the fat left in the frying pan and cook gently for a few minutes. Slowly stir in the red wine, water and seasoning to taste. Bring to the boil, stirring, then pour over the turkey.

4 Cover the casserole tightly and cook in the oven at 150°C (300°F) mark 2, for about 2 hours.

5 Thirty minutes before the end of the cooking time, melt the remaining butter and oil in a frying pan. Add the onions and cook slowly until golden brown and tender. Add the onions to the casserole, cool for 2–3 hours, then chill in the refrigerator until required.

6 Place the casserole on top of the cooker, slowly bring to the boil, then lower the heat and simmer for 20 minutes.

7 Alternatively, reheat in the oven at 220°C (425°F) mark 7 for 30 minutes or until boiling, then at 150°C (300°F) mark 2 for 20 minutes. Garnish with parsley and pastry crescents or croûtons and serve hot.

CASSEROLED TURKEY IN RED WINE

Small pickling onions and shallots are not always easy to obtain all year round, yet they do look attractive whole in this casserole. If you are unable to get them, use 2 medium onions, skinned and chopped, and fry them with the diced bacon in step 2 of the recipe. To improve the appearance of the finished dish, add 100–175 g (4–6 oz) whole button mushrooms in step 5 instead of the whole onions.

VEAL CHOPS WITH SPINACH PURÉE

1.30* 🍳 £ £ 320 cals

* plus overnight marinating

Serves 6

6 veal chops, weighing about 175 g
  (6 oz) each, trimmed

finely grated rind of 2 lemons

90 ml (6 tbsp) lemon juice

150 ml ($\frac{1}{4}$ pint) dry Vermouth

1 large garlic clove, skinned and
  crushed

salt and freshly ground pepper

225 g (8 oz) fresh spinach, trimmed

50 g (2 oz) butter or margarine

freshly grated nutmeg

45 ml (3 tbsp) vegetable oil

bunch of spring onions, trimmed
  and cut into 2.5 cm (1 inch)
  strips

1 egg, hard-boiled and finely
  chopped

1 Place the chops in a large
shallow dish. Whisk together
the lemon rind and juice,
Vermouth, garlic and salt and
pepper to taste. Pour over the
chops. Cover and leave to
marinate in the refrigerator
overnight.

2 Wash the spinach well in
several changes of cold water.
Put in a saucepan with just the
water that clings to the leaves,
cover and cook for 3–4 minutes.

3 Drain the spinach well in a
colander, pressing with the
back of a wooden spoon to extract
as much liquid as possible. Chop
finely.

4 Melt 25 g (1 oz) of the butter in
the rinsed-out pan, add the
chopped spinach and the nutmeg
and cook for 1–2 minutes to dry
off any excess moisture. Transfer
to a bowl, cool and cover.

5 Remove the chops from the
marinade (reserving the
marinade), drain and pat dry with
absorbent kitchen paper. Melt the
remaining butter with the oil in a
large frying pan. When foaming,
add the chops 1 or 2 at a time and
brown well on both sides. Place in
a single layer in a shallow
ovenproof dish.

6 Pour the reserved marinade
into the frying pan. Bring to
the boil, stirring any sediment
from the base. Strain over the
chops. Cover tightly and cook in
the oven at 180°C (350°F) mark 4
for about 50 minutes, or until the
chops are tender.

7 Transfer the chops to a
warmed serving dish and keep
hot. Pour the pan juices into a
blender or food processor, add the
spinach mixture and work until
smooth. Pour into a small
saucepan and simmer gently for
5–10 minutes until hot.

8 Garnish the chops with the
spring onions and chopped
egg. Serve immediately, with the
spinach purée handed separately.

GUINEA FOWL WITH GRAPES

| 1.00 | 🍴 | £ £ | 449–545 cals |

Serves 4

350 g (12 oz) seedless white grapes

30 ml (2 tbsp) brandy

1 garlic clove, skinned and finely sliced

rosemary sprigs

salt and freshly ground pepper

2 prepared guinea fowl

4 streaky bacon rashers, rinded

50 g (2 oz) butter

200 ml (7 fl oz) dry white wine

watercress, to garnish

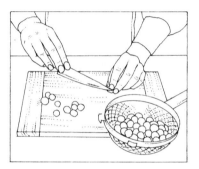

1 Blanch the grapes in boiling water for 2 minutes, then remove skins with a sharp knife.

2 Put the grapes in a bowl. Spoon over the brandy and leave to marinate, turning from time to time.

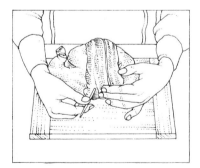

3 Put a few garlic slices, a sprig of rosemary and seasoning inside each bird. Wrap two bacon rashers round each one and secure with wooden cocktail sticks.

4 Place the guinea fowl in a casserole with the butter. Season and sprinkle with a little extra rosemary. Cover and cook in the oven at 220°C (425°F) mark 7 for 15 minutes.

5 Bring the wine to the boil in a pan. Turn the guinea fowl over and pour over the wine. Cook, uncovered, for a further 15 minutes until the birds are tender.

6 Remove the guinea fowl to a warmed serving dish and keep hot. Add the grapes to the sauce and heat through.

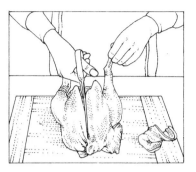

7 Remove the bacon and cut the guinea fowl in half with game scissors. Arrange the bacon over the halves, pour the sauce over and garnish with watercress.

ROAST PHEASANT WITH HERBY FORCEMEAT BALLS

| 1.15 | £ £ | 860 cals |

Serves 4

2 young pheasants, plucked and drawn
150 g (5 oz) butter
10 ml (2 tsp) dried thyme
salt and freshly ground pepper
4 rashers of smoked streaky bacon
450 ml (¾ pint) giblet or chicken stock
225 g (8 oz) pork sausagemeat
50 g (2 oz) fresh white breadcrumbs
finely grated rind of ½ a lemon
25 g (1 oz) shredded suet
15 ml (1 tbsp) chopped fresh parsley
15 ml (1 tbsp) chopped fresh lemon thyme, or 10 ml (2 tsp) dried
15 ml (1 tbsp) chopped fresh sage
1 onion, skinned and finely chopped
1 egg, beaten

1 Wash the inside of the pheasants, then dry with absorbent kitchen paper. Put 15 g (½ oz) butter and 5 ml (1 tsp) thyme inside each bird. Season the birds inside with salt and pepper, then truss with string and/or skewers.

2 Brush the breast of each bird with 25 g (1 oz) softened butter and sprinkle with salt and pepper.

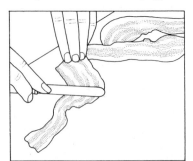

3 Stretch the bacon rashers with the flat of a knife blade, then use two rashers to cover each pheasant breast.

4 Stand the pheasants on a rack in a roasting tin, then pour the stock under the rack. Roast in the oven at 200°C (400°F) mark 6 for 25 minutes.

5 Meanwhile, make the herby forcemeat balls. Mix the sausagemeat, breadcrumbs, grated lemon rind, suet and herbs together until well combined.

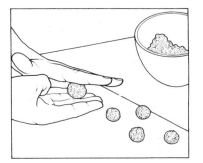

6 Melt 50 g (2 oz) butter in a small pan, add the onion and fry gently for 5 minutes until soft. Mix into the sausagemeat, add salt and pepper to taste, then bind with the beaten egg. Form the mixture into small balls by rolling it in your hands.

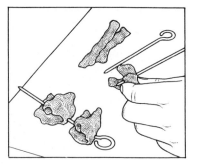

7 Remove the bacon rashers from the pheasants, roll them up and pierce them on to small metal skewers. Arrange on the rack around the pheasants, together with the forcemeat balls.

8 Return to the oven and roast for a further 20 minutes until the pheasants feel tender when pierced in the thickest part of the thighs with a skewer. Serve hot, with gravy made from the stock.

PHEASANT

Only young pheasants are suitable for roasting if the meat is to be tender and moist. Fresh birds are usually sold in a brace, i.e. one cock and one hen together. The cock is the most handsome of the two birds, with his long sweeping tail, green and rust plumage and bright green head crest. The hen pheasant is rather a dull brown, and smaller in size. When looking for young birds, check that the breast is firm and rounded and that the feathers are smooth, with tender wing tips. Check also that the legs are smooth and feet supple; the spurs should have rounded ends—long, sharp spurs are a sign of age.

Frozen pheasants are ready for cooking after defrosting—allow a full 24 hours in the refrigerator—but a fresh pheasant will need hanging, plucking, drawing and trussing beforehand—ask your dealer or butcher to do this for you. If you are going to stuff the bird, as in this recipe, then he can omit the trussing as you will have to do this after the bird has been stuffed.

When serving a brace of pheasant for 4 people, remember to give each person meat from both birds—the hen has moister flesh with a more delicate flavour than the cock.

Traditional accompaniments to roast pheasant are game chips, redcurrant jelly, brussels sprouts and chestnuts and bread sauce.

ROAST DUCK WITH APPLE STUFFING

2.30–3.00*	£ £	610 cals

* plus 15 minutes cooling

Serves 4

15 g ($\frac{1}{2}$ oz) butter

1 celery stick, trimmed and finely chopped

2 small onions, skinned and chopped

100 g (4 oz) fresh white breadcrumbs

1 small eating apple, peeled, cored and grated

15 ml (1 tbsp) chopped fresh sage or 5 ml (1 tsp) dried

salt and freshly ground pepper

1 egg, beaten

2 kg (4 lb) oven-ready duck (with giblets)

1 bay leaf

15 ml (1 tbsp) plain flour

watercress, to garnish

1 Melt the butter in a saucepan, add the celery and half of the chopped onions and fry gently until soft but not brown.

2 Put the breadcrumbs, apple and sage into a bowl and add the softened celery and onion. Mix very well together, add salt and pepper to taste, then bind with the beaten egg. Cool for 15 minutes.

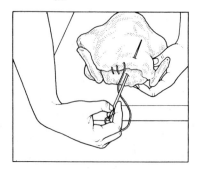

3 Stuff the neck cavity of the duck with this mixture, then sew or truss it together to keep in the stuffing. (If there is too much stuffing for the duck, make the rest into small balls.)

4 Weigh the stuffed duck and calculate the cooking time, allowing 30–35 minutes per 450 g (1 lb). Put the duck on a wire rack in a roasting tin — duck is very fatty and this stops it cooking in its own fat.

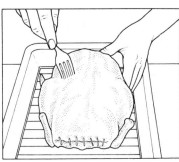

5 Prick the skin of the duck all over to let the fat escape and sprinkle the breast with salt and pepper. Roast in the oven at 180°C (350°F) mark 4 for the calculated cooking time. Cook the stuffing balls in a separate tin on the oven shelf below the duck for the last 30 minutes.

6 While the bird is cooking, make the gravy. Put the giblets in a saucepan with the remaining chopped onion, 600 ml (1 pint) water, the bay leaf and salt and pepper. Simmer for 1 hour; strain.

7 When the duck is cooked, remove from the tin and keep warm in a low oven. Pour off any excess fat from the tin, leaving behind the sediment and about 30 ml (2 tbsp) fat. Transfer to the top of the cooker and blend in the flour. Cook until browned, stirring continuously and scraping any sediment from the bottom of the tin. Slowly stir in the giblet stock and bring to the boil, stirring. Taste and adjust seasoning.

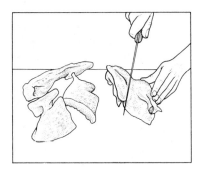

8 To serve, joint the duck into 4 portions, arrange on a warmed serving dish, with the stuffing balls if there are any. Pour the gravy round and garnish with sprigs of watercress. Serve immediately.

ROAST DUCK WITH APPLE STUFFING

It was the Chinese who first discovered how delicious ducks were to eat, and who first bred the white, or Peking, duck for the table. Now ducks are farmed all over the world, and the duck breeding industry is enormous. Of all the duck breeds, it is the English Aylesbury duck which is the most famous. The Aylesbury duck is believed to be a strain of the original Peking duck, taking its name from the Vale of Aylesbury in Buckinghamshire, where it was originally bred. If you see Aylesbury duckling for sale, then you can be sure of buying a good-quality, meaty bird; the flesh will be tender, and the flavour superb.

BOUILLABAISSE

| 0.40 | £ | ✳ | 432 cals |

Serves 6

900 g (2 lb) fillets of mixed white fish and shellfish such as whiting, conger eel, monkfish and prawns

2–3 onions, skinned and sliced

1 stick of celery, washed and chopped

150 ml ($\frac{1}{4}$ pint) olive oil

225 g (8 oz) tomatoes

pared rind of 1 orange

2 garlic cloves, crushed

bay leaf

2.5 ml ($\frac{1}{2}$ tsp) dried thyme

few parsley sprigs

salt and freshly ground pepper

pinch of saffron strands

whole prawns, to garnish

1 Wash the fish and pat it dry with absorbent kitchen paper. Remove any skin, then cut fish into fairly large, thick pieces.

2 Lightly fry the sliced onions and chopped celery in the oil in a large, heavy-based saucepan for 5 minutes or until soft. Skin and slice the tomatoes.

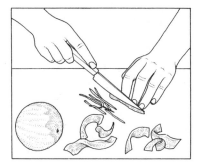

3 Finely shred the orange rind, then stir half into the onion and celery with the garlic, herbs, salt and pepper. Dissolve the saffron in a little hot water.

4 Put the fish in with the vegetables. Add the saffron water and just enough cold water to cover. Bring to the boil and simmer, uncovered, for 8 minutes.

5 Add the prawns and cook for a further 5–8 minutes. Garnish with prawns and remaining rind.

USING SAFFRON
Saffron strands are the dried stigma of the autumn flowering crocus. Although they are very expensive to buy (saffron is the most expensive spice in the world), always use them in recipes like this one which calls for saffron water.

HOT FISH TERRINE WITH GRUYÈRE SAUCE

| 2.15 | £ £ | 549 cals |

Serves 6

75 g (3 oz) butter

1 garlic clove, skinned and crushed

60 ml (4 tbsp) plain flour

750 ml (1¼ pints) milk

550 g (1¼ lb) hake fillets, skinned
and chopped

150 ml (5 fl oz) double cream

10 ml (2 tsp) anchovy essence

3 eggs

1 egg yolk

salt and freshly ground pepper

30 ml (2 tbsp) chopped parsley

125 g (4 oz) shelled prawns,
chopped

125 g (4 oz) Gruyère cheese, grated

watercress sprigs and 6 whole
prawns, to garnish

1 Lightly butter and base line a
1.6-litre (2¾-pint) shallow loaf
tin or terrine. Make sure not to use
too much butter.

2 Melt 40 g (1½ oz) butter in a
saucepan. Add garlic. Stir in
45 ml (3 tbsp) flour and cook for
2 minutes. Remove from the heat
and gradually stir in 450 ml (¾
pint) milk. Bring to the boil,
stirring. Simmer for 2 minutes.

3 In a blender or food processor,
purée the sauce, raw chopped
fish, cream, anchovy essence, eggs
and yolk. Season lightly.

4 Spoon half the fish mixture
into the tin. Sprinkle with
parsley and half the prawns.
Spoon in the rest of fish mixture.
Cover tightly with buttered
greaseproof paper.

5 Place in a roasting tin with hot
water to come halfway up the
sides of the terrine. Cook in the
oven at 150°C (300°F) mark 2 for
about 1¾ hours.

6 Just before the terrine is
cooked, make the sauce. Melt
25 g (1 oz) butter in a pan. Stir in
15 ml (1 tbsp) flour and cook for
2 minutes.

7 Remove from the heat and
gradually stir in the remaining
milk. Bring to the boil, stirring.
Simmer for 2 minutes. Off the
heat, stir in the grated cheese and
remaining prawns. Season to taste.

8 Invert the terrine on to a warm
serving dish and tilt slightly to
drain off juice. Remove cooking
container. Spoon a little sauce over
terrine and garnish with watercress and prawns. Serve the rest
separately.

STUFFED PAUPIETTES OF SOLE

| 1.05 | £ £ | 482 cals |

Serves 6

18 lemon sole quarter-cut fillets
(two from each side of fish)

75 g (3 oz) butter

½ onion, peeled and chopped

225 g (8 oz) button mushrooms,
wiped and trimmed

75 g (3 oz) fresh white breadcrumbs

finely grated rind of 1 lemon

15 ml (1 tbsp) chopped fresh
tarragon leaves

salt and freshly ground pepper

300 ml (½ pint) dry white wine

150 ml (¼ pint) water

30 ml (2 tbsp) plain flour

about 90 ml (6 tbsp) double cream,
at room temperature

fresh tarragon sprigs, to garnish

1 Skin the fillets of sole. Hold each fillet flesh side uppermost at the tail end (dipping your fingers in a little salt helps grip the slippery skin).

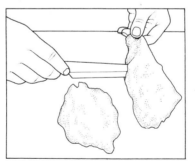

2 Using a sharp knife and a sawing action, work away from you to remove the skin. Wash fish.

3 Make the stuffing. Melt 25 g (1 oz) of the butter in a sauce-pan. Add the onion and fry gently until lightly coloured.

4 Meanwhile, slice half the mushrooms and chop the remainder very finely. Put the chopped mushrooms in a bowl with the breadcrumbs, lemon rind and tarragon.

5 Add the softened onion and season to taste; stir well until the mixture clings together.

6 Place a sole fillet, skinned side uppermost, on a board. Put a teaspoonful of stuffing on one end of fillet. Roll fish up around it. Secure with a cocktail stick.

7 Stand in an upright position in a well-buttered baking dish. Repeat with remaining sole fillets, placing them side by side in dish.

8 Mix together the wine and water and pour over the fish. Cover loosely with foil and bake in the oven at 190°C (375°F) mark 5 for 15 minutes.

9 Remove the fish from the cooking liquid with a slotted spoon and discard the cocktail sticks. Place the fish in a single layer in a warmed serving dish, cover and keep warm. Strain the liquid into a jug.

10 Melt 25 g (1 oz) butter in a saucepan, sprinkle in the flour and cook for 1–2 minutes, stirring. Remove from the heat then gradually stir in the strained cooking liquid. Bring to the boil, reduce the heat and simmer gently for 5 minutes, stirring until thick.

11 Meanwhile, melt the re-maining butter in a frying pan, add the finely sliced mush-rooms and fry gently.

12 Whisk the cream into the sauce. Pour a little sauce over each paupiette; then garnish with sliced mushrooms and tarra-gon sprigs. Pour any remaining sauce into a warmed sauceboat.

CREAMED SEAFOOD VOL-AU-VENTS

| 0.55* | ✳* | 684 cals |

* plus cooling and overnight chilling of filling; freeze filling at the end of step 5

Serves 4

450 g (1 lb) monkfish or haddock fillets

1 bay leaf

few black peppercorns

few parsley sprigs

1 slice of onion

300 ml ($\frac{1}{2}$ pint) milk

25 g (1 oz) butter or margarine

25 g (1 oz) flour

150 ml ($\frac{1}{4}$ pint) single cream

100 g (4 oz) Gruyère cheese, finely grated

1.25 ml ($\frac{1}{4}$ tsp) ground mace or grated nutmeg

salt and freshly ground pepper

225 g (8 oz) prawns, defrosted and thoroughly dried if frozen

16 medium-sized (6.5 cm/$2\frac{1}{2}$ inch) frozen vol-au-vent cases

beaten egg, to glaze

1 Put the monkfish or haddock in a saucepan with the bay leaf, peppercorns, parsley and onion. Pour over the milk, then bring to the boil. Cover tightly, remove from the heat and leave until cold.

2 Remove the fish from the cooking liquid and reserve. Flake the flesh of the fish roughly, discarding the skin and any bones. Set aside.

3 Melt the butter or margarine in a heavy-based saucepan. Sprinkle in the flour and cook, stirring, for 1–2 minutes.

4 Remove from the heat and stir in the strained cooking liquid a little at a time, whisking vigorously until smooth. Simmer gently for 2 minutes, then add the cream and 75 g (3 oz) of the Gruyère cheese. Stir over very low heat until the cheese has melted.

5 Turn the sauce into a bowl and add the mace or nutmeg and seasoning to taste. Gently fold in the flaked white fish and the prawns. Cover the surface of the sauce closely with cling film, leave until cold, then chill overnight.

6 Place the frozen vol-au-vent cases on a dampened baking sheet and brush the rims carefully with beaten egg. Bake in the oven at 220°C (425°F) mark 7 for about 15 minutes or according to packet instructions.

7 Meanwhile reheat the filling gently in a heavy-based saucepan until hot and bubbling. Taste and adjust seasoning.

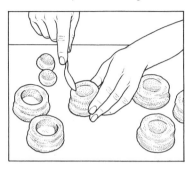

8 Remove the soft centres from the vol-au-vent cases, spoon in the filling, then replace the crisp tops. Serve piping hot.

CREAMED SEAFOOD VOL-AU-VENTS

Frozen uncooked vol-au-vent cases, available at supermarkets and freezer centres, are an absolute boon to the busy cook, because you can quite literally take them from the packet and pop them in the oven—and you get perfectly shaped and beautifully risen vol-au-vents every time. Different manu-facturers sell different sizes, so you must check carefully before buying. Cocktail vol-au-vents are usually about a bite-sized 5 cm (2 inches) in diameter, medium size are 6.5 cm ($2\frac{1}{2}$ inches), large are 9 cm ($3\frac{1}{2}$ inches), and king size are 9.5 cm ($3\frac{3}{4}$ inches). The medium size are the ones most widely available, and the ones to use for most main course dishes—allow four per serving. Large and king size vol-au-vents, while a good size for individual servings, are sometimes difficult to obtain.

BAKED FENNEL

1.30 £ 112 cals

Serves 6

700 g (1½ lb) Florence fennel

salt and freshly ground pepper

75 g (3 oz) butter

finely grated zest of 1 large
 thin-skinned lemon and 30 ml
 (2 tbsp) fresh lemon juice

1 Trim the base and top stems of the fennel, reserving some of the feathery green tops. Quarter each head lengthwise. Blanch in boiling salted water for 5 minutes.

2 Melt the butter in a shallow flameproof casserole. Remove from the heat, and then add the lemon zest together with the lemon juice. Season.

3 Arrange fennel in the casserole in a single layer and turn in the butter. Cover tightly with lid or kitchen foil and bake in the oven at 150°C (300°F) mark 2 for about 1¼ hours. Garnish with snipped fennel tops. Serve hot.

FENNEL
Prized for its unusual aniseed flavour, fennel is called Florence fennel after the Italian city of that name – the Italians are very fond of this vegetable, which grows prolifically all over the Mediterranean. It is the bulb of the vegetable which is used in this recipe, although the leaves of the herb fennel and its seeds are also used in cooking, particularly with fish.

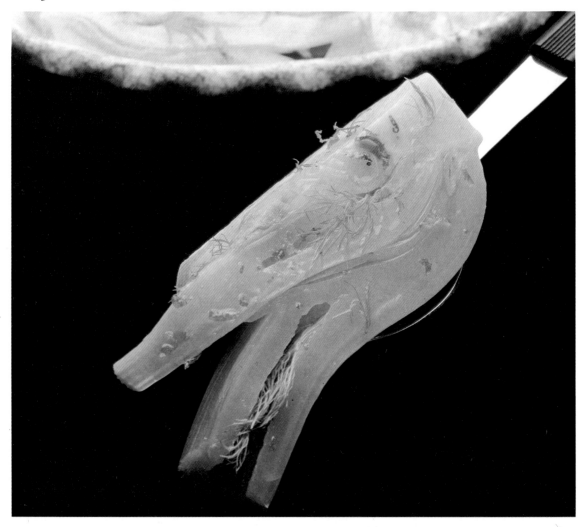

CREAMED BROCCOLI BAKE

| 1.30 | £ | 220 cals |

Serves 6

700 g (1½ lb) broccoli

450 ml (¾ pint) milk

salt and freshly ground pepper

50 g (2 oz) butter or margarine

60 ml (4 tbsp) plain flour

1.25 ml (¼ tsp) grated nutmeg

2 eggs, separated

25 g (1 oz) fresh white breadcrumbs

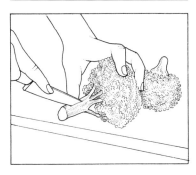

1 Trim and discard any thick broccoli stems; cut up the florets into small pieces, then wash and drain well.

2 Place the broccoli in a medium saucepan with the milk and seasoning and bring to the boil. Cover the pan tightly and simmer gently for 10–15 minutes.

3 Strain off the milk and reserve; finely chop the cooked broccoli. Rinse out and dry the saucepan, then melt the butter and stir in the flour. Cook for 1–2 minutes. Gradually stir in the reserved milk (there should be about 300 ml [½ pint]), season well and bring to the boil, bubble for 2 minutes, stirring.

4 Remove from the heat, beat in the chopped broccoli, nutmeg and egg yolks, and adjust seasoning according to taste.

5 Whisk the egg whites until stiff, and fold into the sauce. Spoon into a well greased 1.4-litre (2½-pint) shallow ovenproof dish.

6 Scatter the breadcrumbs over the top, and bake in the oven at 170°C (325°F) mark 3 for about 50 minutes or until the topping has just set. Serve immediately.

SALSIFY AU GRATIN

| 0.45* | £ | ✳ | 316 cals |

* plus 30 minutes cooling

Serves 4

450 g (1 lb) salsify, trimmed and peeled

300 ml (½ pint) chicken stock

25 g (1 oz) butter

45 ml (3 tbsp) plain flour

2.5 ml (½ tsp) mustard powder

175 g (6 oz) mature Cheddar cheese, grated

salt and freshly ground pepper

50 g (2 oz) fresh breadcrumbs

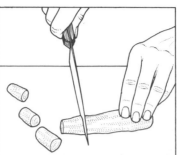

1 Cut the salsify into 2.5 cm (1 inch) lengths and place in a saucepan with the stock.

2 Bring to the boil, cover and simmer gently for 15–20 minutes until tender. Drain, reserving the stock, and place the salsify in an overproof dish.

3 Melt the butter in a saucepan, add the flour and mustard powder and cook over low heat, stirring with a wooden spoon, for 2 minutes. Remove the pan from the heat and gradually blend in the reserved stock, stirring after each addition to prevent lumps forming.

4 Bring to the boil slowly, then simmer for 2–3 minutes, stirring. Add half the cheese and seasoning to taste and pour over the salsify.

5 Mix the remaining cheese with the breadcrumbs and sprinkle over the dish. Cool for 30 minutes, cover and chill in the refrigerator until required.

6 Uncover and bake in the oven at 190°C (375°F) mark 5 for 20–25 minutes until the top is golden brown. Serve hot.

SALSIFY AU GRATIN

Salsify is an inexpensive winter vegetable. It looks rather like a long, thin parsnip, and has a soft, white flesh. Years ago it used to be nicknamed the 'vegetable oyster', because its flavour was thought to be similar to that of oysters. Try coating chunks of salsify in batter after parboiling, then deep-frying them as a tasty alternative to chips.

GREEN BEANS WITH COCONUT

0.15* £ 165 cals

* 8 minutes if using mange-tout

Serves 6

700 g (1½ lb) fresh or frozen green beans or mange tout

salt

1 onion, skinned

50 g (2 oz) butter or margarine

50 g (2 oz) desiccated coconut

freshly ground pepper

45 ml (3 tbsp) chopped fresh parsley

1 Cook the beans in boiling salted water for 10 minutes, or 3 minutes for fresh mange tout (for frozen vegetables, follow packet instructions), until cooked but firm to the bite.

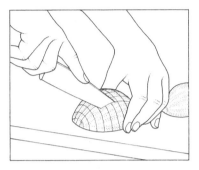

2 Meanwhile, finely chop the onion. Heat the butter in a small frying pan, add the onion and cook gently until softened, stirring occasionally.

3 Increase heat, add coconut and fry for 2–3 minutes until golden. Season and mix in parsley. Drain beans and spoon into a serving dish and sprinkle over coconut mixture.

COCONUT
Desiccated coconut is used in this recipe, but if you can buy a fresh coconut, then so much the better. Simply pierce a hole in its shell and drain off the milk, then crack the shell open with a hammer and dig out the flesh. Grate the flesh finely on a conical or box grater – you will find it far sweeter and juicier than desiccated coconut. Shredded coconut, which comes in large flakes, can also be used if your prefer: it is available at health food shops.

CITRUS SOUFFLÉ

1.30* £ £ ✳ 290–386 cals

* plus 4 hours setting

Serves 6–8

finely grated rind and juice of 1
  lemon

finely grated rind and juice of 1
  orange

juice of 1 grapefruit

15 ml (3 tsp) gelatine

4 eggs, separated

100 g (4 oz) caster sugar

300 ml (10 fl oz) double cream

crushed sweet biscuits and
  crystallised oranges and
  lemons, to decorate

1 Prepare an 18-cm (6-inch)
soufflé dish. Cut a double
thickness of greaseproof paper
long enough to go around the outside of the dish and 5–7.5 cm (2–3
inches) deeper. Secure around the
outside with paper clips and
string.

2 Pour the fruit juices into a
heatproof bowl and sprinkle in
the gelatine. Stand the bowl over a
saucepan of hot water and heat
gently until dissolved. Remove the
bowl from the water and set aside
to cool for 45 minutes.

3 Put the fruit rinds, egg yolks
and sugar in a large heatproof
bowl and stand over the pan of
gently simmering water. Whisk
until the mixture is thick and
holds a ribbon trail.

4 Remove the bowl from the pan
and whisk in the gelatine
liquid. Leave until beginning to
set, whisking occasionally.

5 Whip the cream until it will
stand in soft peaks. Whisk the
egg whites until stiff. Fold the
cream into the soufflé, then the
egg whites, until evenly blended.

6 Pour the mixture into the prepared soufflé dish and level the
surface. Chill in the refrigerator
for at least 4 hours until set.

7 Carefully remove the paper
from the edge of the soufflé.
Press the crushed biscuits around
the exposed edge, then decorate
the top with crystallised fruit.
Serve chilled.

─── VARIATIONS ───

Children love the zingy flavour of
this soufflé, and if you don't want
to go to the trouble of preparing a
soufflé dish with a collar, it can be
set in a serving bowl like a mousse.
Ring the changes with the flavour
according to the fruit available—
make it with just oranges and
lemons if you like, or with just one
citrus fruit. For an extra special
dinner party, add a spoonful or
two of orange-flavoured liqueur.

DEVIL'S FOOD CAKE

| 2.00* | 🍽 | ✳* | 696 cals |

* plus 30 minutes cooling and 1 hour standing time; freeze after stage 8

Serves 8

75 g (3 oz) plain chocolate plus 25 g (1 oz) (optional)

250 g (9 oz) soft light brown sugar

200 ml ($\frac{1}{3}$ pint) milk

75 g (3 oz) butter or block margarine

2 eggs

175 g (6 oz) plain flour

3.75 ml ($\frac{3}{4}$ tsp) bicarbonate of soda

450 g (1 lb) caster sugar

120 ml (8 tbsp) water

2 egg whites

1 Lightly brush two 19-cm ($7\frac{1}{2}$-inch) sandwich tins with melted lard. Base-line with grease-proof paper and grease the paper. Leave for 5 minutes to set, then dust with sugar and flour.

2 Break 75 g (3 oz) of the chocolate in small pieces into a saucepan. Add 75 g (3 oz) of the brown sugar and the milk. Heat very gently, stirring to dissolve the sugar and blend the ingredients, then remove from the heat and leave to cool for 10 minutes.

3 Put the butter into a bowl and beat until pale and soft. Gradually add the remaining brown sugar and beat until pale and fluffy.

4 Lightly whisk the eggs and gradually beat into the creamed mixture. Slowly add the cooled chocolate mixture beating until combined.

5 Sift the flour and bicarbonate of soda into the creamed mixture and gently fold in using a metal spoon. Turn the mixture into prepared tins, then tap gently to level it.

6 Bake in the oven at 180°C (350°F) mark 4 for about 35 minutes. The cakes are cooked when they spring back when pressed lightly with a finger and have shrunk away a little from the sandwich tins.

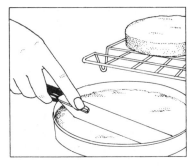

7 Cool in the tins for a couple of minutes before turning out on to a wire rack to cool completely. Ease them away from the tins using a palette knife, taking care not to break the crust.

8 Tap the tins on the work surface to loosen the cakes. Gently pull off the paper and leave to cool.

9 Put the sugar for the frosting in a pan with the water, dissolve over a low heat, then boil rapidly to 115°C (240°F) on a sugar thermometer, or until the mixture reaches the soft ball stage. Check by plunging a teaspoonful into a bowl of iced water. It should form a ball in your fingers.

10 Meanwhile, whisk the egg whites in a large bowl until stiff. Allow the bubbles in the syrup to settle, then slowly pour the hot syrup on to the egg whites, beating constantly. Once all the sugar syrup is added, continue beating until the mixture stands in peaks and just starts to become matt round the edges. (The icing sets quickly, so work rapidly.)

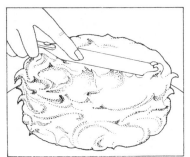

11 Sandwich the cakes together with a little of the frosting. Spread the remaining frosting over the cake with a palette knife. Pull the icing up into peaks all over, then leave the cake for about 30 minutes, to allow the icing to set slightly.

12 Break up the chocolate, if using, and put it in a small bowl over a pan of hot water. Heat gently, stirring, until the chocolate has melted. Dribble the chocolate over the top of the cake with a teaspoon to make a swirl pattern. Leave for 30 minutes before serving.

AMERICAN CAKES

Two classic cakes from America are Angel Food Cake and Devil's Food Cake. The first is an airy vanilla-flavoured sponge. It is very white in colour and light in texture because it is made with flour and egg whites, with no egg yolks. Its opposite number is the rich, moist chocolate cake recipe given here. Generously filled and coated with frosting, Devil's Food Cake is a favourite for serving as a dinnertime dessert, or at coffee parties.

DOBOS TORTE

| 2.10 | 🍴 🍴 | £ | 655 cals |

Serves 8

4 eggs

275 g (10 oz) caster sugar

150 g (5 oz) plain flour

100 g (4 oz) plain chocolate

3 egg whites

175 g (6 oz) icing sugar

225 g (8 oz) butter

50 g (2 oz) crushed biscuits or
chopped nuts, to decorate

1 Line two baking sheets with non-stick paper. Put the whole eggs into a heatproof bowl with 175 g (6 oz) caster sugar and place over simmering water, whisking until the mixture is thick enough to leave a trail on the surface when the whisk is lifted, then remove from the heat.

2 Sift half the flour over the mixture and fold in lightly with a metal spoon. Add the remaining flour in the same way.

3 Carefully spread some of the mixture out on the baking sheets in large rounds measuring about 20 cm (8 inches) in diameter. Bake in the oven at 190°C (375°F) mark 5 for 7–10 minutes until golden brown.

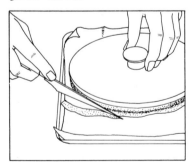

4 Loosen from the baking sheets and trim each round to a neat shape with a sharp knife, using a saucepan lid as a guide. Transfer them on to wire racks and leave for about 15 minutes to cool.

5 Re-line the baking sheets, spread on more mixture. Bake, trim and cool as before. There will be enough mixture to make six or seven rounds.

6 Select the round with the best surface and lay it on an oiled baking sheet.

7 Put the remaining caster sugar in a small, heavy based saucepan. Over a gentle heat, dissolve the sugar, without stirring, and boil it steadily to a rich brown.

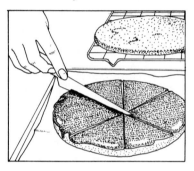

8 Pour it over the round on the baking sheet, spreading it with a knife brushed with oil. Mark into eight sections and trim round the edge.

9 Break the chocolate into a heatproof bowl and place over simmering water. Stir until the chocolate is melted, then remove from the heat.

10 Put the egg whites and icing sugar into a heatproof bowl and place over simmering water Whisk until very thick, then remove from the heat.

11 Put the butter into a bowl and beat until pale and soft. Beat the egg and sugar mixture into it gradually, then stir in the melted chocolate.

12 Sandwich the remaining biscuit rounds together with some of the filling and put the caramel-covered one on top.

13 Spread the sides of the torte with more filling and press the crushed biscuit crumbs or chopped nuts round the sides.

14 Spoon the remaining filling into a piping bag fitted with a star nozzle and pipe a decorative border round the top edge.

— VARIATION —

For a simpler filling, melt 50 g (2 oz) plain chocolate as above and leave to cool slightly. Cream 150 g (5 oz) butter and gradually beat in 225 g (8 oz) sifted icing sugar. Beat in the melted chocolate while it is still soft.

DOBOS TORTE

The old Austro-Hungarian empire is the home of this elaborate 'drum cake'. Versions of the traditional sponge rounds, layered with chocolate cream and glazed with caramel, are still to be found in the best cafés and pastry shops from Vienna to Budapest.

Be sure to mark the caramel into portions before it hardens or it will be extremely difficult to cut.

COFFEE CHEESECAKE

1.00*	✳	380 cals

* plus 2–3 hours chilling

Serves 8

50 g (2 oz) butter, melted

175 g (6 oz) gingernut biscuits, finely crushed

15 ml (1 tbsp) gelatine

45 ml (3 tbsp) cold water

15 ml (1 tbsp) instant coffee powder

30 ml (2 tbsp) coffee-flavoured liqueur

300 ml (½ pint) boiling water

150 g (5 oz) soft brown sugar

450 g (1 lb) curd cheese

300 ml (10 fl oz) whipping cream

coffee beans, to decorate

1 Lightly oil a 20-cm (8-inch) loose-bottomed deep cake tin or spring-release cake tin.

2 Stir the butter into the crushed biscuits. Press firmly into the base of the tin. Refrigerate for 30 minutes until set.

3 Sprinkle the gelatine on to the cold water. Leave to soak for 10 minutes.

4 Stir the coffee and coffee liqueur into the boiling water. Add the soaked gelatine, stirring until dissolved. Stir in the sugar.

5 Put the coffee mixture and curd cheese into a blender and work until just smooth. Leave until beginning to set then lightly whip the cream and fold half into the cheese mixture.

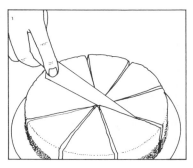

6 Turn the mixture into the prepared tin and refrigerate for 2–3 hours or until set. When set, remove from the tin. To serve, cut into eight, pipe a cream whirl on top of each slice and decorate with coffee beans.

ALTERNATIVE DECORATIONS

For even better effect, buy sugar coffee beans, available from high-class confectioners. Alternatively, thin chocolate leaves or squares would look attractive and taste good.

VACHERIN AU CHOCOLAT ET AUX MARRONS

(CHOCOLATE AND CHESTNUT MERINGUE GÂTEAU)

2.00* 🔲 🔲	468–561 cals

* plus cooling and chilling

Serves 10–12

175 g (6 oz) shelled hazelnuts

6 egg whites

350 g (12 oz) caster sugar

225 g (8 oz) dark or bitter chocolate

60 ml (4 tbsp) dark rum

350 g (12 oz) sweetened chestnut
   purée (from a can or tube)

300 ml (½ pint) double or whipping
   cream

chocolate caraque or grated
   chocolate, to decorate

1 Grease and base-line three
   20.5 cm (8 inch) sandwich tins.

2 Toast the hazelnuts lightly
   under the grill, shaking the
pan frequently.

3 Transfer the nuts to a clean
   tea-towel and rub gently while
still hot to remove the skins.
Grind until very fine.

4 Put the egg whites in a large
   bowl and beat until very stiff
and standing in peaks. Beat in half
of the sugar until the meringue is
glossy. Fold in the remaining
sugar with the hazelnuts.

5 Spoon the meringue into the
   prepared sandwich tins. Level
the tops and bake in the oven at
180°C (350°F) mark 4 for 35–40
minutes until crisp.

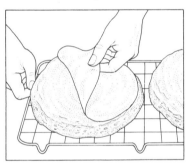

6 Invert the tins onto a wire rack
   and turn out the meringues.
Peel off the lining papers carefully. (Do not worry if the
meringues are cracked, this will
not show in the finished dessert.)
Leave to cool.

7 Break the chocolate in pieces
   into a heatproof bowl standing
over a saucepan of gently
simmering water. Add the rum
and heat gently until the chocolate
has melted, stirring only once or
twice after the chocolate has
started to melt. Remove from the
heat and gradually blend in 225 g
(8 oz) of the chestnut purée.

8 Put 1 meringue round, soft
   side uppermost, on a serving
plate. Spread with half of the
chocolate and chestnut mixture,
then top with the second meringue
round, crisp side uppermost.
Spread with the remaining mixture
then top with the last round.

9 Whip the cream until it holds
   its shape. Reserve 30 ml
(2 tbsp) of the cream and swirl the
remainder all over the gâteau to
cover the top and sides completely.
Blend the remaining chestnut
purée into the reserved cream,
then pipe around the edge.
Decorate with chocolate. Chill in
the refrigerator.

Apfel Strudel

2.45* 🍴 🍴 £ 321–401 cals

* plus 1 hour standing time
Serves 8–10

225 g (8 oz) plain flour
2.5 ml ($\frac{1}{2}$ tsp) salt
1 egg, slightly beaten
30 ml (2 tbsp) vegetable oil
60 ml (4 tbsp) lukewarm water
45 ml (3 tbsp) seedless raisins
45 ml (3 tbsp) currants
75 g (3 oz) caster sugar
2.5 ml ($\frac{1}{2}$ tsp) ground cinnamon
1 kg (2$\frac{1}{4}$ lb) cooking apples, peeled, cored and grated
45 ml (3 tbsp) melted butter
100 g (4 oz) ground almonds
icing sugar, to decorate

1 Lightly oil a baking sheet. Put the flour and salt into a large bowl, make a well in the centre and pour in the egg and oil.

2 Add the water gradually, stirring with a fork to make a soft, sticky dough. Work the dough in the bowl until it leaves the sides, then turn it out on to a lightly floured surface and knead for about 15 minutes.

3 Form into a ball, place on a cloth and cover with a warmed bowl. Leave to 'rest' in a warm place for 1 hour. Put the raisins, currants, sugar, cinnamon and apples into a bowl and mix together thoroughly.

4 Warm the rolling pin. Spread a clean cotton cloth on the table and sprinkle lightly with 15–30 ml (1–2 tbsp) flour.

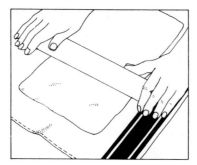

5 Place the dough on the cloth and roll out into a rectangle about 3 mm ($\frac{1}{8}$ inch) thick, lifting and turning it to prevent sticking.

6 Gently stretch the dough, working from the centre to the outside, until it is paper-thin.

7 Trim the edges to form a rectangle about 68.5 × 61 cm (27 × 24 inches). Leave the strudel dough on the cloth to dry and 'rest' for 15 minutes.

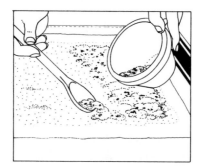

8 Position the dough with one of the long sides towards you, brush with melted butter and sprinkle with ground almonds.

9 Spread the apple mixture over the dough, leaving a 5-cm (2-inch) border uncovered all round the edge. Fold these pastry edges over the apple mixture, towards the centre.

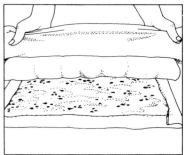

10 Lift the corners of the cloth nearest to you over the pastry, and roll up the strudel. Stop after each turn to pat into shape and to keep the roll even.

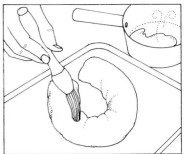

11 Form the roll into a horseshoe shape, slide it on to the prepared baking sheet and brush it with melted butter.

12 Bake in the oven at 190°C (375°F) mark 5 for about 40 minutes or until golden brown. Dredge the strudel with icing sugar. Serve hot or cold, in slices, with cream.

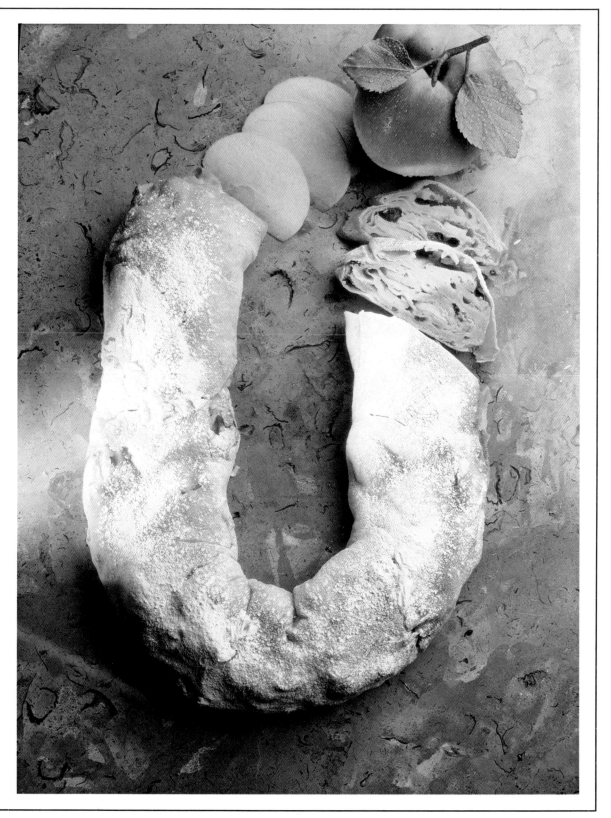

WALNUT MERINGUE TART

| 0.55* | 🍳 | £ | 475–658 cals |

* plus 30 minutes chilling and 1 hour cooling

Serves 4–6

50 g (2 oz) butter or block margarine

175 g (6 oz) light soft brown sugar

1 egg yolk

100 g (4 oz) plain flour

2 egg whites

2.5 ml (½ tsp) vanilla flavouring

100 g (4 oz) walnuts, chopped

whipped cream, to serve

1 Melt the fat, cool for 5 minutes, then stir in 25 g (1 oz) of the sugar with the egg yolk and flour. Knead lightly, then press over the base and up the sides of a greased pie plate measuring 21.5 cm (8½ inches) across the top. Refrigerate for 30 minutes.

2 Whisk the egg whites in a clean, dry bowl until stiff, but not dry. Gradually whisk in the remaining sugar, keeping mixture stiff. Add the vanilla flavouring with the last spoonful of sugar.

3 Fold in the chopped walnuts, then spoon into the pastry-lined pie plate.

4 Bake in the oven at 180°C (350°F) mark 4 for 30 minutes until the filling is well risen. Cool completely for 1 hour. As the meringue cools it will shrink and crack slightly.

5 Serve the walnut tart cold, cut in wedges, with whipped cream over the top.

PANCAKES CREOLE

0.45*	🍳 £ £ ✳*
405–553 cals	

* not including making the pancake batter; freeze cooked pancakes only

Serves 4–6

pancake batter made with 300 ml (½ pint) milk

finely grated rind and juice of 1 lime

50 g (2 oz) butter or margarine

50 g (2 oz) demerara sugar

60 ml (4 tbsp) dark rum

2.5 ml (½ tsp) ground cinnamon

3–4 bananas

orange and lime, to decorate

1 Make 8–12 pancakes in the usual way. Slide each pancake out of the pan on to a warm plate and stack with greaseproof paper in between.

2 Put the lime rind and juice in a saucepan with the fat, sugar, rum and cinnamon. Heat gently until the fat has melted and the sugar dissolved, stirring occasionally.

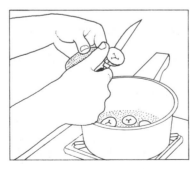

3 Peel the bananas and slice thinly into the sauce. Cook gently for 5 minutes until tender.

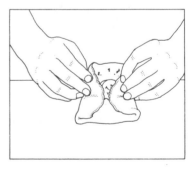

4 Remove the banana slices from the sauce with a slotted spoon. Place a few slices in the centre of each pancake, then fold the pancakes into 'envelopes' around the cooked bananas.

5 Place in a warmed serving dish and pour over the hot sauce. Decorate with orange and lime twists and serve with cream, if liked.

CHARLOTTE RUSSE

1.35* ⊟ ⊟ f 447 cals

* plus 50 minutes cooling and 4 hours
setting

Serves 6

135-g (4¾-oz) packet lemon jelly,
   broken into squares

about 450 ml (¾ pint) boiling water

45 ml (3 tbsp) lemon juice

2 glacé cherries, quartered

piece of angelica, cut into triangles

300 ml (½ pint) milk

1 vanilla pod

45 ml (3 tbsp) water

15 ml (3 tsp) gelatine

3 egg yolks

45 ml (3 tbsp) caster sugar

about 18 sponge fingers

300 ml (10 fl oz) whipping cream

1 Dissolve the jelly in a
measuring jug, according to
the packet instructions, using the
lemon juice and enough boiling
water to make 600 ml (1 pint).
Cool for 20 minutes. Spoon a thin
covering of cool jelly into the base
of a 1.1-litre (2-pint) charlotte tin;
refrigerate for about 20 minutes or
until set.

2 When set, arrange the cherry
quarters and angelica triangles
on top. Carefully spoon over cool
liquid jelly to a depth of about
2.5 cm (1 inch). Refrigerate for
about 30 minutes to set, together
with the remaining jelly.

3 Bring the milk slowly to the
boil with the vanilla pod; take
off the heat, cover and leave to
infuse for at least 10 minutes. Put
the water in a small bowl and
sprinkle in the gelatine. Stand the
bowl over a saucepan of hot water
and heat gently until dissolved.
Remove the bowl from the water
and set aside to cool slightly.

4 Using a wooden spoon, beat
together the egg yolks and
sugar until well mixed, then stir in
the strained milk. Return to the
pan and cook gently, stirring all
the time until the custard is thick
enough to just coat the back of the
spoon—do *not* boil. Pour into a
large bowl, stir in the gelatine and
allow to cool for 30 minutes.

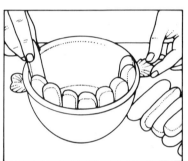

5 Trim the sponge fingers so
that they just fit the tin; reserve the trimmings. Stand the
fingers closely together, sugar side
out, around the edge of the tin.

6 Lightly whip the cream and
stir into the cool custard. Place
the bowl in a roasting tin. Pour in
enough iced water to come halfway up its sides. Stir occasionally
for about 10 minutes until the
custard is on the point of setting
and has a *thick* pouring con-
sistency. Pour gently into the lined
mould without disturbing the
sponge fingers.

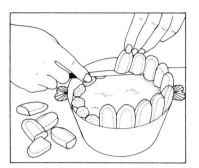

7 Trim the sponge fingers level
with the custard. Lay the trimmings together with the reserved
trimmings on top of the custard.
Cover with cling film and refrigerate for at least 3 hours to set.

8 To turn out, using fingertips,
ease the sponge fingers away
from the tin, then tilt it slightly to
allow an airlock to form between
the two. Dip the base of the tin in
hot water for about 5 seconds
only—to loosen the jelly. Invert
the pudding on to a damp plate,
shake tin gently, then ease it carefully off the finished charlotte.

9 Loosen the remaining set jelly
by dipping the jug in hot water
for a few seconds only. Turn out
on to a board lined with damp
greaseproof paper. Moisten a
large knife and chop the jelly into
small pieces. Spoon the jelly
around the charlotte russe.

CHARLOTTE RUSSE

A classic French dessert, this
charlotte Russe (Russian
charlotte) is made with a filling
of *crème bavarois*—a rich vanilla-
flavoured egg custard. Sometimes the custard is flavoured
with chocolate, almond-
flavoured liqueur or kirsch.
Fresh raspberries can also be
added when they are in season.

CRÈME BRÛLÉE

1.25* 🍴 £ £ 423 cals

* plus 1 hour cooling and 4–6 hours chilling

Serves 6

600 ml (20 fl oz) whipping cream

4 egg yolks

100 g (4 oz) caster sugar

5 ml (1 tsp) vanilla flavouring

1 Put the cream in the top of a double saucepan or in a heat-proof bowl over a pan of hot water. Heat gently; do not boil.

2 Meanwhile, put the egg yolks, 50 g (2 oz) of the caster sugar and the vanilla flavouring in a bowl and beat thoroughly. Add the cream and mix well together.

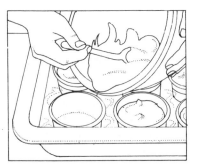

3 Stand six individual ramekin dishes in a roasting tin, then pour in enough hot water to come halfway up the sides of the dishes. Pour the custard mixture slowly into the ramekins, dividing it equally between them.

4 Bake in the oven at 150°C (300°F) mark 2 for about 1 hour or until set, then remove from tin and cool for 1 hour.

5 Refrigerate for 2–3 hours, preferably overnight. Sprinkle the top of each crème brûlée with the remaining sugar and put under a preheated hot grill for 2–3 minutes until the sugar turns to caramel. Refrigerate again for 2–3 hours before serving.

PRUNE AND PORT FOOL

| 0.45* | £ | ✳ | 433 cals |

* plus overnight soaking and 2 hours chilling

Serves 4

100 g (4 oz) stoned prunes, soaked overnight in cold water

50 g (2 oz) caster sugar

60 ml (4 tbsp) port

finely grated rind and juice of 1 medium orange

150 ml ($\frac{1}{4}$ pint) thick custard, cooled

150 ml (5 fl oz) double cream

sweet biscuits, to serve

1 Drain the prunes, then put in a saucepan with the sugar, port, orange rind and juice. Simmer for about 15 minutes until soft. Leave to cool slightly, then purée in a blender or food processor. Leave to cool completely.

2 Fold the cooled custard into the puréed prunes. Whip the cream until it will stand in soft peaks, then fold into the prune custard until evenly blended.

3 Divide the mixture between four individual glasses, then chill in the refrigerator for about 2 hours until firm. Serve chilled, with sweet biscuits.

RUM TRUFFLES

| 0.25* | £ £ | 103 cals |

* plus 30 minutes setting time and
  30 minutes chilling

Makes 12–14

125 g (4 oz) plain chocolate
12.5 ml (2½ tsp) rum
1 egg yolk
25 g (1 oz) cake crumbs
25 g (1 oz) icing sugar
chocolate vermicelli

1 To make the truffle mixture, melt the chocolate in a small bowl over a pan of hot water and add the rum. It is important that the mixture doesn't get too hot. When melted, stir in the egg yolk and cook, stirring all the time, until the truffle mixture begins to thicken very slightly.

2 Remove the bowl from the heat and gently stir in the cake crumbs and icing sugar. Continue stirring until mixture cools a little.

3 Place the prepared truffle mixture in the refrigerator and leave for about 30 minutes until it is almost set.

4 Divide the mixture into twelve pieces. With a little icing sugar on your hands, roll the mixture into balls. Roll each ball in the vermicelli and place in individual paper cases.

5 Store, covered, in the refrigerator. Take out of the refrigerator about 30 minutes before serving.

TURKISH DELIGHT

| 0.45* | ▯ ▯ | £ | 74 cals |

* plus 24 hours cooling

Makes about 550 g (1¼ lb)

300 ml (½ pint) water
25 g (1 oz) gelatine
450 g (1 lb) granulated sugar
1.25 ml (¼ tsp) citric acid
few drops of vanilla flavouring
few drops of almond flavouring
few drops of red and green food
  colouring
few drops of red food colouring
50 g (2 oz) icing sugar
25 g (1 oz) cornflour

1 Have ready a 20.5 × 15-cm (8 × 6-inch) tin. Put the water in a heavy-based saucepan. Sprinkle the gelatine over it, add the sugar and citric acid and heat slowly until the sugar has dissolved. Bring to the boil and boil for 20 minutes.

2 Remove from the heat and leave to stand for 10 minutes without stirring. Add the flavourings and a few drops of food colouring and pour the mixture into the dampened tin. Leave in a cool place for 24 hours.

3 Sift the icing sugar and the cornflour together and sprinkle them evenly over a piece of greaseproof paper.

4 Turn the Turkish delight out on to the paper and cut it into 48 squares with a sharp knife. Toss in sugar mixture, then pack in greaseproof paper and store in an airtight tin.

ALMOND STARS

| 0.40 | £ £ | ✳ | 110 cals |

Makes about 24

2 egg whites
150 g (5 oz) ground almonds
75 g (3 oz) caster sugar
few drops of almond flavouring
24 pieces of angelica or glacé
  cherries, to decorate

1 Line two baking sheets with greaseproof paper. Whisk the egg whites until stiff and use a tablespoon to fold in the almonds, sugar and almond flavouring.

2 Using a large star vegetable nozzle, pipe the almond-flavoured stars, quite close together, on to the lined baking sheets.

3 Decorate each star with a piece of angelica or a glacé cherry. Bake in the oven at 150°C (300°F) mark 2 for 15–20 minutes until just beginning to colour.

PETITS FOURS

Petits fours are the delicious, rich little sweets and biscuits that are served with coffee after dinner.

Traditional petits fours often include little iced cakes made from a Genoese sponge mixture cut into small shapes – triangles, squares, rounds or shapes cut with small fancy cutters. They are coated with apricot jam and then covered with fondant, marzipan or glacé icing. They may be decorated with nuts, glacé fruits, or crystallised flowers.

INDEX

GOOD HOUSEKEEPING

...For the life women <u>REALLY</u> lead

Dear Reader,

We do hope you will enjoy your **Good Housekeeping** cookery book and will go on to collect the other titles available from your **BP Service Station.** Each recipe given has been double tested for success by our highly respected and unique resource, the **Good Housekeeping Institute,** so you can try new dishes with complete confidence.

It is that same confidence and trust that makes millions of women read our **Good Housekeeping** magazine each month. Colourful and glossy, it is always brimming over with new and exciting ideas, plus practical advice on a huge range of topics that affect all our everyday lives. No wonder so many people now subscribe to **Good Housekeeping** each month to ensure they don't miss a single copy.

Uniquely for BP customers we are offering a special introductory rate to all new UK subscribers of only £11.20 — *a saving of £2 on the current rate!* **For this amount you will receive a copy of Good Housekeeping by post each month for 12 months.**

Credit card holders can order by telephoning 0444 440421 or by post to the address below.

Happy reading!

Brian Braithwaite

Brian Braithwaite
Publishing Director — Good Housekeeping

Subscription enquiries and orders with payment to:
Quadrant Subscription Services, FREEPOST, Haywards Heath, West Sussex RH16 3ZA.
Offer closes 31st August 1989.

IMPORTANT: TO QUALIFY FOR YOUR DISCOUNT QUOTE "SAK" IN ALL COMMUNICATIONS.

Published by Ebury Press
Division of The National Magazine Company Ltd
Colquhoun House
27–37 Broadwick Street
London W1V 1FR

The Good Housekeeping Institute is the food and consumer research centre of
Good Housekeeping magazine.
Printed and bound in Italy by New Interlitho, S.p.a., Milan